# Kris Kringle's
# CHRISTMAS
# CANDY
# COOKBOOK

## *Grandma Kate*

SMITHMARK

*This book is dedicated to my children, Sherrie and Steven. Their sticky fingers, sweet kisses and satisfied grins made it seem like Christmas all year long. And to all with whom I share my recipes, may you enjoy Christmas cheer year 'round with lots of sticky fingers, sweet kisses and satisfied grins.*

This edition published in 1993 by
SMITHMARK Publishers Inc.
16 East 32nd Street, New York, NY 10016

SMITHMARK books are available for bulk purchase
for sales promotion and premium use.
For details write or call the manager of special sales,
SMITHMARK Publishers Inc.,
16 East 32nd Street, New York, NY 10016; 212-532-6600.

Produced by
Wieser & Wieser, Inc.
118 East 25th Street, New York, NY 10010

Editor: Jake Elwell
Designer: Tony Meisel
Photographer: Melanie Acevedo

Printed in Hong Kong

10 9 8 7 6 5 4 3 2 1

ISBN 0-8317-5164-9

# CONTENTS

Rudolf's Salt Water Toffee

# INTRODUCTION

Candy canes, Christmas trees and snowballs . . . reminders of Christmas.

Generations of families have made candy at Christmas time to give as gifts and to share when family and friends come to visit. This book is about sharing those gifts. Women have traditionally shared their skills from quilt making to cooking. These recipes are from at least five generations. Take a look at homemade candy canes—beautiful as Tiffany glass plus that wonderful peppermint taste. Imagine these on an old fashioned Christmas tree reflecting the light from real candles and the squeals of delight as the children pick one from the tree to eat.

These recipes represent five generations in my family and they may have come from your family's yesteryears.

*Christmas Trees*

# TIPS FOR BETTER CANDY

CORN SYRUP: Corn syrup is an important ingredient in making candy. It is used to help prevent large sugar crystals from forming and to insure a smooth texture.

SUGAR: Whether the sugar you are using comes from sugar beets or sugar cane makes no difference. Either will give successful results in my candy recipes.

COOKING STAGES: If you are using a CANDY THERMOMETER, cook your candy to the exact temperature called for by the recipe (subtract two to four degrees if you're cooking in altitudes above 3,000 feet) Especially with creamy candies, the only sure way to know when the candy is done is to use a candy thermometer.

If you do not have a candy thermometer, the COLD WATER TEST is the next best thing (I've used it for years). Drop about 1/2 teaspoon of cooking candy mixture into about 1 cup cold water. Be sure the water is very cold. Let it stand about one minute and check the firmness of the mass with your fingers. Remove the candy from the heat while making the test so as not to over cook.

If you are using the cold water test, use these guidelines for the cooking stages: SOFT BALL stage means that when your candy mixture is placed in cold water you can pick up the mixture and form it into a soft, pliable ball. It will hold its shape in the pliable ball stage. The HARD BALL stage means that when your candy mixture is placed in cold water you can pick up the mixture and form a ball that becomes hard within seconds. It does not remain pliable. The CRACK STAGE means that when your candy mixture is poured into the cold water, it will immediately shatter and you will hear a cracking noise. You cannot form this mixture into a ball. The HARD CRACK or BRITTLE stage means that not only will you hear the mixture crack when placed in cold water, but it is so brittle it will shatter into small pieces when you pick it up. Be sure to cook your candy to the proper stage otherwise your candy will not set up properly.

Use the following table to convert back and forth between thermometer instructions and cold water method instructions, depending on the recipe and the method you prefer:

| COLD WATER STAGE | EQUIVALENT TEMPERATURE |
|---|---|
| "Soft ball" | 234°-240° |
| "Hard ball" | 250°-266° |
| "Crack" or "Soft crack" | 270°-290° |
| "Hard crack" or "brittle" | 300°-310° |

OVERCOME GRAININESS: Once a spoon is used to mix and dissolve sugar, rinse the spoon thoroughly and dry. It is also good to rinse the spoon after a cold water test, especially if the mixture is stirred infrequently.

DO NOT SHORT CUT COOLING PERIOD: With creamy candies be sure to cool cooked mixture to 110 degrees F. before starting to beat. Do not move or jar saucepan. If mixture is stirred while hot, candy becomes grainy. DO NOT SCRAPE PAN. Leavings may be sugary. Pour out quickly. If mixture becomes too stiff to turn into the pan, try a little hot water, milk or cream (1/2 teaspoon at a time) until candy is the right consistency.

FONDANT: The word "fondant" is sometimes used instead of the word "mixture". Fondant is a smooth, creamy candy. It can be used as a filling for candies or fruits, or rolled, sliced and served as is. In this book you'll find recipes for "fancy" fondants, delicious treats in their own right.

Peppermint Candy Canes

# CANDY CANES

Christmas trees and candy canes—we couldn't have Christmas without them!

I have continued a very old family tradition of putting homemade candy canes on the tree and letting holiday visitors pick their own. Be careful, though, you may find your guests leaving with more than one cane in hand and sheepish grins on their faces.

## *Peppermint Candy Canes*

*2 cups sugar*
*1/2 cup light corn syrup*
*1/2 cup water*
*1/4 teaspoon cream of tartar*
*3/4 teaspoon peppermint extract*
*3/4–1 teaspoon red or green food coloring*

Combine sugar, corn syrup, water and cream of tartar. Stir until sugar dissolves. Cook without stirring to a very hard crack stage. Remove from heat and add peppermint extract. Divide into 2 portions.

Add red or green coloring to one part. Pour a strip of clear candy mixture onto a well greased surface. Make the strip approximately 18" long, 1" wide and 5/8" deep.

Pour a strip of colored candy mixture onto the well greased surface and next to the clear candy strip. Make the colored strip the same length and depth but 3/4" wide. Cool two or three minutes—only until you can handle the candy and it is pliable.

Immediately place the colored strip on top of the clear strip. The colored strip will not be as wide as the clear strip. Cut in strips 6" long. Twist 1 to 1 1/2 turns. Do not twist tight. The strip must be a spiral formation. Turn the top of each cut strip down to make the hook or top of the candy cane. Place the candy canes on a cake rack several inches apart in a very cool, dry place. To remove the moisture from the canes place the rack of canes in front of a fan in a cool, dry place for at least 8 hours. When canes are completely dry, they may be placed in the freezer.

# Barber Pole Candy Canes

*1 large egg white*
*1/2 tablespoon cold water*
*1/2 teaspoon peppermint extract*
*2 cups sifted confectioners' sugar*
*Red food coloring (see below)*

Combine egg white, water and peppermint extract. Beat with electric beater. When well beaten (approximately 4 minutes), slowly add the sugar. Continue beating. Beat until mixture is stiff. Place the mixture on a board that has been covered with powdered sugar. Knead until smooth.

Take 1/2 of mixture and roll into a long roll that is 1/2 of the thickness desired for candy cane thickness. Add red food coloring to remainder of mixture to desired color. Separate the red mixture into halves. Roll out each half until very thin. Place on each side of white roll. Twist the three rolls. Roll the entire roll until smooth. Cut to desired length of cane. Turn down the top to form the hook of the candy cane. Let dry thoroughly. May be frozen.

Just like candy canes at the dimestore, only homemade!

# FANCY FONDANTS

These Parisian Sweets are delectable and delightful for any age and any occasion from a swank dinner party to a midnight snack. Wrapped in pretty foil they make great stocking stuffers as well as a welcome treat for Santa!

## *Yuletide Cream Fondant*

*4 cups sugar*
*1/8 teaspoon cream of tartar*
*2 cups thin cream*
*2 teaspoons light corn syrup*
*Peppermint or vanilla extract, if desired*

Combine sugar and cream of tartar in a large, heavy saucepan. Blend thoroughly. Gradually add cream and corn syrup. Blend thoroughly. Place over low heat. Stir until sugar is dissolved and mixture is boiling gently. Cover. Cook for 3 minutes. Remove cover. If crystals form a ring during the cooking process, remove with a damp cloth wrapped around the tines of a fork.

Cook without stirring to a firm ball stage. Pour candy mixture at once into a large, cold-water-rinsed platter or large oven glass baking pan—do not scrape saucepan. Cool candy to lukewarm without disturbing it. Beat with wooden spoon or spatula. Candy will begin to harden gradually. At this stage, push candy together in center of platter or pan with hands or spatula. It will harden rapidly and become very firm.

Cover candy closely with a damp cloth. Let stand 1 1/2 hours. Remove cloth. Break off small quantity of firm candy and knead with the hands until all the lumps have disappeared and the candy is smooth and pliable. If desired, add extract, a few drops at a time, kneading it thoroughly into candy. Repeat until the entire mass has been kneaded and flavored. Form a 2"x12" roll. Wrap tightly with foil, waxed paper or plastic wrap. Place in refrigerator. Use as desired.

# Pulled Mints

2 cups sugar
3/4 cup water
1/4 cup butter
2 tablespoons light corn syrup
3/4 teaspoon peppermint extract
1 1/2 cups sifted powdered sugar

Combine sugar, water, butter and syrup. Blend thoroughly. Place over low heat. Stir until sugar is dissolved and mixture is boiling gently. Cover. Cook 3 minutes. Remove cover. Cook without stirring to hard ball stage. If crystals form on sides of pan during cooking process, remove with damp cloth wrapped around tines of a fork. Remove from heat. Pour at once onto lightly oiled platter. Add flavoring. Do not stir.

As soon as candy is cool enough to handle, pull until light and fluffy. Stretch into long rope. Cut in 1-inch pieces with a sharp knife. Place on waxed paper to dry. When mints are thoroughly dry, dust with powdered sugar. Cover with remaining powdered sugar. Place in airtight container. Cover top of container with cloth which has been wet and wrung quite dry. Place lid tightly over cloth. Mints require at least two days to ripen and become creamy. Turn or shake mints once or twice during ripening process to prevent sticking. If cloth becomes dry, dampen again.

# Stuffing for Dates

These stuffings may be eaten by themselves. They are delicious fondant candy that is light and creamy. Color the fondant to suit any holiday or party decoration scheme. Most seedless dates are sold slit and ready for stuffing.

ORANGE-PEANUT STUFFING: To 1/3 cup (1/4 pound) peanut butter slowly add 5 tablespoons of orange juice (1/2 medium orange) and 1/2 teaspoon grated orange rind or a tablespoon chopped candied orange peel. Stuff dates. These dates may be sprinkled with chopped salted peanuts.

North Pole Wintergreen Mints

APRICOT-COCONUT STUFFING: Wash 1 cup (1/3 pound) dried apricots. Place in a colander or wire strainer over boiling water for 5 minutes to soften. Run through a food chopper alternately with 1/2 cup nut meats and 2/3 cup shredded coconut. Add 2 tablespoons orange juice and 1 teaspoon grated orange rind.

Mix with hands until well blended. Stuff dates and roll in sugar.

## Parisian Date Sweets

*1 package (10 ounce) dates*
*1 package (1/4 pound) shredded coconut*
*1/2 cup chopped nuts*
*1/2 pound figs or 1/4 pound figs and 1/4 pound dried apricots*
*1 tablespoon orange juice*
*1 teaspoon orange rind or chopped candied orange peel*

Run the dates, figs, apricots and coconut through the food chopper. Knead in the orange juice and rind. Divide into four parts. Stuff dates. May also be rolled in sugar. Makes 1 1/2 pounds.

## Orange Fondant

*1 egg yolk*
*1 cup confectioners sugar*
*1–2 tablespoons grated orange rind*
*1 1/2 tablespoons orange juice*

Beat egg yolk slightly. Stir in the confectioners sugar, adding orange juice to make fondant of proper consistency for stuffing. Add grated orange rind. The egg yolk serves to color the fondant. It may be omitted if additional orange juice and orange vegetable coloring are used. This recipe will be sufficient for a one pound package of dates.

# North Pole Wintergreen Mints

In double boiler, combine 2 cups sifted confectioners sugar, 6 1/2 teaspoons water and 1/4 teaspoon wintergreen extract. Add red or green food coloring to desired hue. Cook until mixture loses its gloss and becomes dull. Immediately drop by teaspoonfuls onto waxed paper or press into candy mold as I have done. Makes about 2 dozen.

*Apricot Snowballs*

# FRUIT CANDY

My mother was always after us to eat our spinach, peas and other such "good" food. We also learned that some food could be "good for you" and delicious. Some of it was even *candy*! Your kids too will be surprised to learn these treats are not only tasty, they are healthy as well.

## *Apricot Snowballs*

Wash and dry 24 dried apricots. Put through food chopper together with 1 1/2 cups shredded coconut. Add 2 teaspoons orange juice and 2 tablespoons confectioners sugar. Blend well. Shape into 3/4 inch balls. Roll in fruit sugar. Makes 2 dozen.

## *Cherry Puffs*

2 1/2 cups sugar
1/2 cup water
2 egg whites
2/3 cup light corn syrup
1/4 teaspoon salt
1/2 teaspoon vanilla
1 cup candied cherries

Slice the candied cherries as desired. In a saucepan, cook the sugar, syrup, salt and water, stirring until the sugar is completely dissolved. Continue cooking without stirring until hard ball stage is reached. If any sugar crystals form on the sides of the pan, wash them away with a piece of wet cheesecloth wrapped around the tines of a fork.

Remove from heat and gradually pour the syrup over the egg whites, which have been beaten stiff during the latter part of the cooking of the syrup. Beat during this addition. Continue beating until the candy will hold its shape when dropped from a spoon. Add vanilla and cherries. Mix thoroughly. Drop by teaspoonfuls on waxed paper. This candy is attractive when colored a delightful pink. (Cold water test: hard, almost brittle stage). Makes 1 1/3 pounds.

# Date Kisses

2 egg whites
1/4 teaspoon salt
3/4 cup sugar
3/4 cup chopped dates
1 cup chopped pecans
1 teaspoon vanilla

Beat egg whites and salt until they hold a peak. Gradually add sugar, beating constantly. Fold in chopped dates, nuts and vanilla. Drop from teaspoon about an inch apart onto well greased cookie sheet. Bake at 325 degrees F. about 35 minutes. Makes 2 1/2 dozen.

# Good-for-you Prune Sweets

1/4 pound sweet chocolate
2 cups cooked, pitted prunes
3/4 cup seedless raisins

Melt the chocolate and stir in the raisins. Lay the pitted prunes out flat and drop a spoonful of chocolate on each. Chill.

# Tutti-Frutti Roll

1 cup fine graham cracker crumbs
1/2 cup finely chopped candied cherries
1/4 cup finely chopped candied pineapple
1/2 cup finely chopped marshmallows
1/4 cup finely chopped green maraschino cherries
1/4 cup chopped pecans
1/4 teaspoon nutmeg
1/2 teaspoon cinnamon
1 teaspoon vanilla extract
1/4 cup light cream

Mix all ingredients then shape into 2 rolls, 1 1/2" in diameter. Roll in 1/2 cup fine graham cracker crumbs. Chill. Cut into thin slices.

# FLUFFY COCONUT

When I think of coconut I think of the tropics—until I make Coconut Snowballs. This wonderful candy from Germany sweetened many a household and tastes so good when coming in from throwing "real" snowballs!

## Coconut Snowballs

1/4 cup butter
4 cups confectioners sugar
1/4 cup light cream
1/2 teaspoon vanilla
1 cup shredded coconut

Melt butter. Add sifted sugar alternately with cream and vanilla, stirring well after each addition. Beat until smooth. Sprinkle breadboard or pastry canvas with small amount of confectioners sugar. Turn mixture out on sugared board and knead until smooth and glossy. About ten minutes. Form balls. Roll in coconut. Makes 2 dozen.

## Coconut Drops

2 cups sugar
1/2 cup milk
1 1/2 cups shredded coconut
1/2 teaspoon vanilla

Heat sugar and milk over low heat,, stirring constantly until sugar is dissolved. Increase heat and cook, stirring constantly, until candy reaches a soft ball stage. Remove from heat. Stir in coconut and vanilla. Drop from teaspoon onto a greased baking sheet. Makes 2 pounds.

# Frosty's Coconut Kisses

1 cup sugar
5 tablespoons water
2 egg whites
1/2 pound shredded coconut
1/2 teaspoon salt

Boil sugar and water to soft ball stage. Beat egg whites until stiff. While still beating, slowly add hot syrup. Add coconut and salt. Drop from teaspoon onto well greased cookie sheet. Bake at 250 degrees F. about 45 minutes. Remove from sheet immediately. Makes 2 dozen.

# Coconut Peaks

1/4 cup butter or margarine
2 cups sifted confectioners sugar
1/4 cup light cream
3 cups snipped shredded coconut
1 6-ounce package semisweet chocolate pieces
Green food coloring (for Christmas Tree variation)

In saucepan, slowly heat butter until golden brown; gradually stir in sugar, cream and coconut. If making Christmas Trees (see below), add green food coloring. Drop by teaspoonfuls onto waxed paper. Chill until easy to handle. Then shape into peaks. Stir until smooth. Dip bottom of each peak or Christmas tree into chocolate. Let harden on rack covered with waxed paper. Makes 3 dozen.
CHRISTMAS TREES VARIATION: Use Christmas Tree mold if you have one. If using cookie or candy cutter, lay small Christmas tree cutter on waxed paper. Pack coconut mixture into cutter to depth of 1/2-inch. Lift off cutter. Repeat. Decorate with candied cherry and preserved citron bits. Let harden.

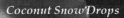
*Coconut Snow Drops*

# PEANUT BUTTER SURPRISES

Here's something else good for you—peanut butter. Try the Peanut Butter–Mashed Potato Mystery Fudge and the Pinwheels. Never has a mashed potato had it so good! You'll like it and so will all the neighborhood kids.

## *Peanut Brittle*

2 tablespoons butter or margarine
1/2 cup boiling water
2 tablespoons molasses
1 1/2 cups granulated sugar
1 cup salted peanuts (rub lightly between paper towels to remove excess salt)
1 teaspoon baking soda

Grease shallow pan. In large heavy skillet, melt butter. Add water and molasses. Add sugar and stir well to dissolve. (If using a candy thermometer, set in place). Bring mixture to boil. Boil without stirring to 310 degrees F., or until a little mixture in cold water becomes very brittle. Remove from heat. Quickly add peanuts and baking soda. Stir until foam is well combined with mixture. Pour into pan. With two forks, pull and stretch candy into thin layer. When cold, break into pieces. Makes 3/4 pound.

## *Prancer's Peanut Crispettes*

3 cups crisp corn flakes
3 cups crisp rice krispies
1 cup salted peanut meats
1 cup sugar
1 cup light corn syrup
1 cup light cream
1 teaspoon vanilla extract

Mix cereals and peanut meats. Combine sugar, syrup and cream in a saucepan and stir. Heat slowly until sugar is dissolved. Boil uncovered to hard boil stage, stirring occasionally. Remove saucepan from heat and add extract. Pour over cereal mixture and mix carefully. Press into a greased pan 9"x12". Cut into squares. If desired, decorate with candied cherries.

## Peanut Butter Balls

Combine 2 cups snipped shredded coconut with 1/2 cup creamy (or chunk style) peanut butter and 4 teaspoons vanilla extract. Mix well. Shape into small balls between the palms of your hands. Arrange on waxed paper in pan. Chill thoroughly. Makes 2 dozen.

## Peanut Butter-Filled Kisses

*1 cup light molasses*
*2/3 cup sugar*
*1/2 cup light corn syrup*
*1/2 cup hot water*
*1/4 teaspoon cream of tartar*
*1/4 cup soft butter or margarine*
*1/2 teaspoon salt*
*1/2 teaspoon vanilla extract*

In a 4 quart saucepan (important if you want to save yourself trouble) mix molasses, sugar, corn syrup, water and cream of tartar. When thoroughly mixed, cook and stir until sugar is dissolved. Continue cooking without stirring to the soft ball stage. Add butter or margarine a little at a time and the salt.

Cook again, this time to the hard ball stage, stirring occasionally to prevent scorching. Remove from heat. Let stand until sputtering stops. Pour a thick layer onto a greased cookie sheet. While candy cools, keep turning the edges towards the center so that cooling is uniform. When it is cool enough to handle, pour in vanilla extract.

Pull until candy turns lighter in color. (It will never pull to the taffy-hard stage). Cut into several pieces. Roll one piece at a time on an ungreased cookie sheet with rolling pin until you have a strip that measures about 4" wide and 1/8" thick. Spoon a generous piping of peanut butter down the center of the strip and overlap sides of candy over peanut butter, making a long, thick roll about 1" in diameter. Cut into individual kisses and wrap in waxed paper, foil or plastic wrap. Makes 2 dozen.

## Peanut Butter–Mashed Potato Mystery Fudge

2/3 cup cold mashed potatoes (without milk or seasoning added)
1/2 cup peanut butter
1/8 teaspoon salt
4 cups sifted confectioners sugar

Grease 2"x8"x2" pan. Mix potatoes with peanut butter and salt. Gradually stir in sugar, mixing well. Press into greased 2"x8"x2" pan. Let stand until firm, then cut. See if folks can guess the *mystery* ingredient!

## Peanut Butter-Potato Pinwheels

1/2 cup cold mashed potatoes (without milk or seasoning added)
1/8 teaspoon salt
4 cups sifted confectioners sugar
1/2 teaspoon vanilla extract
1 cup peanut butter

To potatoes add salt and enough confectioners sugar to make them easy to handle. Beat well. Add vanilla and turn 1/2 of mixture onto board that has been lightly dusted with confectioners sugar. Roll into rectangle 1/4" thick. Spread with half of peanut butter. Roll up from short side, jelly roll fashion. Repeat with remaining mixture. Chill. Slice 1/4" thick. Makes 4 dozen.

*Peanut Brittle*

# DIVINITY

Irish born Divinity Kisses are a blessing from the Emerald Isle. These creations, whose recipes come directly from the old world, are just as suitable for Christmas Day as St. Patrick's Day.

## *Elves' Choice Divinity*

*2 cups sugar*
*1/2 cup light corn syrup or honey*
*1/2 cup water*
*2 egg whites, beaten stiff*
*Pinch of salt*
*1 teaspoon vanilla*
*1/2 cup walnuts or chopped mixed fruit*

Boil sugar, syrup and water to hard ball stage. Add salt to egg whites and beat until stiff. Pour the syrup slowly over the stiffly beaten egg whites. Continue beating until it begins to look dull and gets stiff. Add flavoring and nuts or fruit. Pour into a deep pan, leaving top slightly rough, or drop by spoonfuls on waxed paper.

## *Gaelic Divinity Kisses*

*2 1/2 cups sugar*
*1/2 cup light corn syrup*
*1/2 cup water*
*2 stiffly beaten egg whites*
*1 teaspoon vanilla*
*1/2 cup chopped walnuts (optional)*
*1/2 cup red or green candied cherries*

Cook sugar, corn syrup and water to thin syrup stage. Slowly pour 1/3 over egg whites, beating constantly. Cook remaining syrup to crack stage. Add 1/2 to egg white mixture, beating constantly. Cook remaining syrup to firm ball stage. Add to egg white mixture. Add vanilla. Beat until mixture holds shape when dropped from spoon. Stir in walnuts. Swirl from teaspoon onto waxed paper. Top with cherry half. Makes 4 dozen.

*Caramel Pinwheels*

# CARAMELS GALORE

Every gift box of candy should include caramels. So smooth and delectable. What a treat and what a surprise—no one would expect you to make them yourself!

My Great Grandmother was Queen of the church bazaar with her Caramel Pinwheels—especially delicious with chocolate flavoring added to the cream filling.

## *Caramel Pinwheels*

1 cup sugar
1/3 cup light corn syrup
1 1/2 cups heavy cream
1 teaspoon vanilla
1/2 lb. fondant (see fondant recipes)

Grease a 1" deep oblong pan. Mix sugar, syrup and 1/2 cup cream in a saucepan. Cook over low heat, stirring constantly, until sugar dissolves. Increase heat and bring mixture to a boil. Cook gently, stirring constantly, until candy thermometer registers 234 degrees F., or when a little of the mixture dropped in cold water forms a soft ball.

Add 1/2 cup cream and cook again to a soft ball stage or 234 degrees F., stirring constantly, then add the last 1/2 cup cream and cook, stirring constantly, until thermometer registers 250 degrees F., or mixture forms a hard ball.

Immediately cool by setting pan in cold water. With as little stirring as possible, mix in vanilla. Pour candy into buttered pan. Cool. When caramel is cool but still pliable, cut in half to form two pieces. Place rolls of fondant on the caramel and roll up like a jelly roll. Chill until firm. Cut into 1/4" slices. Makes two 1-pound rolls.

# Java Caramels

2 cups sugar
1/2 cup light corn syrup
1/2 cup strong coffee
1 1/2 cups heavy cream
2 tablespoons butter or margarine
1/4 teaspoon salt
1 teaspoon vanilla extract

In a 2 quart saucepan combine sugar, corn syrup, coffee and half the cream. Cook over medium heat, stirring constantly, until all sugar has been dissolved. Continue cooking without stirring for 15 minutes. Add the remaining cream, butter or margarine and salt. Cook to hard ball stage.

Remove from range. Cool for several minutes. Add vanilla extract and stir gently. Pour into a greased 8" square pan and cool completely. When cold and firm, cut into individual pieces with kitchen scissors. Wrap in waxed paper or plastic wrap or put in foil cups. Makes approximately 4 dozen caramels.

Leave a dish of these for Santa on Christmas Eve to help him stay awake!

# Walnut Caramels

1 cup walnuts
2 cups light corn syrup
1/2 cup butter or margarine
1 (14 ounce) can evaporated milk
1/8 teaspoon salt
2 cups sugar
1 teaspoon vanilla

Chop the walnuts into small pieces. Mix salt and sugar in a heavy saucepan. Cook over low heat, stirring constantly, until sugar is dissolved. Increase heat and cook, stirring constantly until candy thermometer registers 250 degrees F. or mixture forms a hard ball.

Remove from heat and quickly stir in nuts and vanilla. Pour into a buttered square pan. Cool.

When completely cold, remove candy from pan and cut in 1" pieces with a sharp knife. Decorate each caramel with a walnut half. Makes 2 pounds.

For a tasty variation, dip in melted chocolate.

*Butter Crunch*

# CHOCOLATE DELIGHTS

The wonderful taste of chocolate has delighted young and old in our family for generations. French Chocolate Truffles were a favorite of my Grandmother and, quite frankly, a favorite of mine!

## *Bittersweet Balls*

1 12-ounce package semisweet chocolate pieces
3/4 cup evaporated milk
1/2 cup finely chopped walnuts
1/2 cup chocolate sauce

Melt chocolate over hot (not boiling) water. Stir in milk. Cook, stirring frequently, for 20 minutes. Mixture should be thick. Chill 1 hour or until easy to handle. Then shape into 3/4" balls. Roll some in walnuts and some in chocolate sauce. Makes 3 dozen.
VARIATION: Add 1/4 teaspoon cinnamon to mixture.

## *Blitzen's Butter Crunch*

1 cup butter or margarine
1 cup sugar
2 tablespoons water
1 tablespoon light corn syrup
3/4 cup chopped nuts
2 squares semisweet candy-making chocolate or unsweetened chocolate

Melt the butter or margarine in a 2 quart saucepan over low heat. Remove from heat. Add sugar. With a wooden spoon, stir the mixture until well blended. Return to low heat. Stir rapidly until thoroughly mixed and beginning to bubble. Add water and corn syrup. Mix well. Put in candy thermometer. Keep heat low. Stir frequently until brittle stage (approximately 15 to 20 minutes). Remove from heat at once.

   Sprinkle nuts over surface and quickly mix in. Pour onto lightly greased cookie sheet. With spatula spread 1/4" thick. Cool to room temperature. As crunch cools, loosen from sheet with spatula 2 or 3 times. Partially melt 2 squares chocolate over boiling water. Remove from water. Stir until melted. Spread evenly over crunch. Set aside until firm. Turn onto waxed paper or another cookie sheet and spread with melted chocolate. When firm break into pieces.

Store in lightly covered container in a cool place.

## Chocolate Ting-a-Lings

*1 12-ounce package semisweet chocolate pieces*
*1 cup corn flakes*
*1/2 cup snipped shredded coconut*
*1 teaspoon vanilla extract*
*1/2 cup salted peanuts, pitted dates or seedless raisins cut in small pieces*

Melt chocolate over hot (not boiling) water. Stir until smooth. Remove from heat. Stir in corn flakes, coconut, vanilla and peanuts. Drop by teaspoonfuls onto waxed paper. Chill until firm. Makes 2 dozen.
VARIATION: Substitute peanuts with dates or raisins; use white chocolate as I did.

## Chocolate Toffee

*1 cup brown sugar, firmly packed*
*1 cup granulated sugar*
*1/3 cup corn syrup*
*1/2 cup water*
*1/8 teaspoon salt*
*1/2 cup butter*
*1 6-ounce package semisweet chocolate, melted*
*1/2 cup chopped nuts*

Combine sugar, syrup, water and salt in heavy saucepan. Blend thoroughly. Place over medium heat. Stir until sugar is dissolved and is boiling gently. Cook to firm ball stage. Add butter. Continue cooking to hard crack stage. Stir as necessary to prevent burning. Pour into lightly oiled 9" square pan.

Cool until hard and brittle. Spread top with half the melted chocolate. Sprinkle with half the chopped nuts. Place on cooling rack for chocolate to dry. When chocolate is firm turn toffee over. Spread with remaining chocolate and sprinkle with remaining chopped nuts. Let stand until chocolate is firm. Break into various sized pieces.

## Chocolate "Wayside" Bars

*1 cup semisweet chocolate pieces*
*2 tablespoons vegetable shortening*
*1 1/2 cups coarsely crumbled saltines*

Melt chocolate and shortening over hot (not boiling) water. Stir until smooth. Remove from heat. Add saltines. Mix thoroughly. Press into 11"x7"x1 1/2" pan. Mark into squares. Cool until firm. Cut apart. Makes two dozen.

## Heavenly Truffles

*2 12-ounce packages semisweet chocolate pieces*
*3/4 cup sweetened condensed milk*
*Pinch of salt*
*1 cup chopped walnuts or 1 cup chopped candied fruit or raisins (optional)*
*1 teaspoon vanilla extract or 1 tablespoon rum*

In double boiler, melt chocolate over hot (not boiling) water. Stir in condensed milk, salt, chopped nuts and extract. Pour into waxed paper lined 9"x5"x3" loaf pan. Cool for a few hours. When firm cut into squares. Makes 1 1/4 pound.

Let your imagination run wild when decorating truffles as you see I have done with mine—melted chocolate bands of differing colors and assorted hard candies lend variety and holiday color to your candy dish.

## French Chocolate Truffles

Cool Heavenly Truffles mixture until easy to shape into small balls. Dip each ball into snipped shredded coconut, chopped nuts, sweetened cocoa powder or instant coffee powder. Chill.

*Truffles*

# Tannenbaum Peanut Bark

*1 12-ounce package semisweet chocolate pieces*
*5 tablespoons warmed evaporated milk*
*1 cup salted or unsalted peanuts*

Melt chocolate over hot (not boiling) water. Stir until smooth. Remove from heat. Immediately stir in, until blended, milk and peanuts. Pour onto waxed paper. Flatten with spatula. Chill a few minutes or until firm. Cut into irregular pieces. Makes 2 1/2 dozen.

## Fruit or Nut Clumps

Follow Peanut Bark recipe above substituting 1 cup seedless raisins, finely chopped pitted dates, pecan halves or broken walnut meats for peanuts. Drop by teaspoonfuls onto greased cookie sheet. Chill until firm. Makes 2 dozen.

*Tannenbaum Peanut Bark*

# FUDGE

As a modern day mother and grandmother, time is of the essence and my little Five Minute Fudge recipe has "done me proud", saving my neck on many occasions. I was one of the blessed mothers whose children volunteered me for everything—and I never turned them down.

## Cherry-Orange Fudge

*1 1/3 tablespoons butter*
*1 to 2 teaspoons grated orange rind, as desired*
*1 cup thin cream or 2/3 cup evaporated milk plus 1/3 cup water*
*3 cups sugar*
*3/8 teaspoon cream of tartar*
*3 tablespoons orange juice*
*1 teaspoon lemon juice*
*2/3 cup chopped nuts*
*1 (3 ounce) can or jar of red maraschino cherries*

Melt butter in heavy saucepan. Remove from heat. Add orange rind. Blend thoroughly. Add cream or evaporated milk, sugar, cream of tartar and orange juice. Blend thoroughly. Place over low heat. Stir until sugar is dissolved and mixture is boiling gently. Cover. Cook 3 minutes. Remove cover. If crystals form on sides of pan during the cooking process, remove with damp cloth wrapped around tines of fork. Stir occasionally to soft ball stage. Because this is a very soft fudge, it must be cooked at this low temperature.

Remove from heat. Cool at room temperature until lukewarm. Add lemon juice and nuts. Beat until thick and creamy. This candy requires lots of beating. Spread evenly in lightly oiled 8"x8" pan. Cool. Cut in squares. Cut red petals from glossy, outside portion of cherries. Use 3 petals to form each flower. Arrange flower on each piece of candy.

# Grandma Kate's Five Minute Fudge

1 2/3 cups granulated sugar
2 tablespoons butter or margarine
1/2 teaspoon salt
2/3 cup undiluted evaporated milk
1 3/4 package semisweet chocolate pieces (24-ounce size)
1/2 pound marshmallows, diced
3/4 cup chopped walnuts
1 teaspoon vanilla extract

Grease 9"x8"x2" pan. In 2 quart saucepan, combine sugar, margarine, salt and milk. Bring to a boil over medium heat. Boil five minutes, stirring constantly. Remove from heat. Add chocolate, marshmallows, walnuts and vanilla extract. Beat vigorously until marshmallows melt. Pour into pan, sprinkle with more nuts if desired. Cool. Cut into small squares. Makes about 5 dozen.

## Pentagon Fudge

1 3-ounce package cream cheese
2 1/3 cups sifted confectioners sugar
1/2 teaspoon almond extract
1/2 cup chopped almonds
Dash of salt

Grease 9"x5"x3" loaf pan. With electric mixer beat cream cheese until soft and smooth, Slowly blend in sugar, extract, nuts and salt. Pour into pan. Chill until firm. Cut into squares. Makes 2 1/2 dozen.

*Donner's Butterscotch Drops*

# MISCELLANEOUS MUNCHIES

Munchies are so good sitting in front of the fireplace, talking to friends or reading. Munchies are so good you won't be able to stop eating them.

## Almond Squares

2 cups blanched almonds
2 cups sifted confectioners sugar
Rind of 1/2 lemon
2 egg whites

Grind almonds very fine through a food grinder. Be sure the nuts are dry, otherwise you're in for trouble. If they seem moist and oily, spread them over a shallow pan and dry them in a slow oven, 300 degrees F., before grinding. Now put the ground almonds in a large mixing bowl, stir in sugar and lemon rind. Pound hard with the handle of a wooden spoon. Pound about 5 to 7 minutes to get all the flavor mixed through. Add unbeaten egg whites and work the mixture. Place in a square pan and refrigerate.

## Baked Candy Squares

1 egg white unbeaten
1/4 teaspoon salt
1 teaspoon vanilla extract
1 cup light brown sugar, packed
1 cup chopped walnuts

Start heating oven to 350 degrees F. Grease 8"x8"x2" pan. Combine egg white, salt, vanilla extract and brown sugar. Beat well with spoon or electric mixer at high speed one or two minutes or until smooth and fluffy. Stir in walnuts. Spread in pan. Bake 30 minutes. Cool in pan, then cut. Makes 3 dozen. Keeps well in pan.

# Donner's Butterscotch Drops

1/2 cup granulated sugar
1/4 cup white corn syrup
1/4 cup water
1 tablespoon butter or margarine
1/2 teaspoon vanilla extract

In a 2 quart saucepan, combine sugar, corn syrup and water (if using candy thermometer set in place). Cook over low heat, stirring, to 266 degrees F., or until a little mixture in cold water forms a very hard ball. Add butter. Cook to 310 degrees F., or until a little mixture in cold water becomes brittle. Remove from heat. Add vanilla. Drop from teaspoon onto greased cookie sheet. When firm remove with spatula. Makes 2 dozen.

# Mallow Pops

For each pop, stick a marshmallow onto a long kitchen fork. Hold in steam of boiling water until sticky. Drop marshmallow onto finely chopped walnuts, roll over and over until coated. Place on waxed paper until firm. Stick a short, colored straw (red and green are nicest) into each mallow pop.
VARIATION: Can be first dipped in melted semisweet chocolate and then dropped onto finely chopped nuts.

# Nut Crunch

1 1/4 cups granulated sugar
3/4 cup butter or margarine
1/4 cup water
1/2 cup unblanched almonds
1/2 teaspoon baking soda
1/2 cup blanched almonds
1/2 cup chopped walnuts
1/3 cup semisweet chocolate bits
1/2 cup finely chopped nuts

In saucepan mix sugar, margarine, water and almonds. Boil mixture to brittle stage. Stir occasionally. Stir in soda and the almonds and walnuts. Pour into greased pan. Spread with melted chocolate. Sprinkle with finely chopped nuts. Cool. Break up. Makes 1 1/2 pounds.

## *Rudolph's Salt Water Taffy*

*8 cups sugar*
*1 cup light corn syrup*
*1 cup water*
*1 1/2 teaspoon salt*
*2 teaspoons glycerine*
*1 tablespoon butter*
*2 teaspoons vanilla*

In a saucepan, cook all ingredients except butter and flavoring. Stir until sugar is dissolved. If sugar crystals form on the sides of the saucepan during cooking, wash them away with a piece of wet cheesecloth wrapped around the tines of a fork. Continue cooking until the temperature of 260 degrees F. is reached. Remove from fire. Add butter. When butter is melted, pour into a greased pan. When cool enough to handle, gather into a ball and pull until it is rather firm. Add flavoring while pulling. Stretch out in a long rope and cut into pieces of desired size. Usually the pieces of salt water taffy are about 2 inches in length. Wrap in waxed paper or plastic wrap.

Salt Water Taffy can be colored during the pulling. Add coloring to the taffy and pull it through. Color should suit the flavor: wintergreen taffy is usually colored pink; vanilla with white; spearmint with green; cinnamon with red. Rudolph prefers the cinnamon—to match his nose!

## *Maple Pralines*

*2 cups pecans*
*2 cups light brown sugar*
*1 cup maple flavored syrup*
*1/3 cup evaporated milk or cream*

Chop the pecans coarsely. Mix the sugar, syrup and evaporated milk or cream. Heat over low heat, stirring constantly until sugar is dissolved. To remove sugar crystals wipe with a dampened piece of cheesecloth wrapped around tines of a fork. Bring mixture to a boil. Cook without stirring to soft ball stage. Remove from heat. Let stand 5 minutes. Add nuts. Stir until syrup is slightly thick and beginning to appear cloudy. Drop from the tip of a teaspoon onto a greased baking sheet or onto waxed paper, forming patties 2" in diameter. Cool. Remove and store in airtight container. Makes 1 1/2 pounds.

## *Plantation Pralines*

*2 cups sugar*
*1 teaspoon baking soda*
*1 cup buttermilk*
*Pinch of salt*
*2 tablespoons butter or margarine*
*2 1/3 cups pecan halves*
*2/3 cup perfect pecan halves*

In large kettle (about 8 quart) combine sugar, baking soda, buttermilk and salt. Cook over high heat 5 minutes being sure to stir frequently and to scrape bottom and crevices of kettle. Cook to 234 degrees F. Remove from heat. Add butter and 2 1/3 cups pecans. Cook, stirring continuously to soft ball stage. Remove and let stand—just a minute or two. Then with a spoon, beat until thickened and creamy. Immediately drop by tablespoonfuls onto waxed paper, aluminum foil or greased cookie sheet. Dot with 2/3 cup perfect pecans.

Decorated Truffles